March 22 / 2022

I Love My Pet
BIRD

Aaron Carr

www.av2books.com

AV² provides enriched content that supplements and complements this book. Weigl's AV² books strive to create inspired learning and engage young minds in a total learning experience.

Your AV² Media Enhanced books come alive with...

 Audio
Listen to sections of the book read aloud.

 Video
Watch informative video clips.

 Embedded Weblinks
Gain additional information for research.

 Try This!
Complete activities and hands-on experiments.

 Key Words
Study vocabulary, and complete a matching word activity.

 Quizzes
Test your knowledge.

 Slide Show
View images and captions, and prepare a presentation.

... and much, much more!

Go to **www.av2books.com**, and enter this book's unique code.

BOOK CODE

V640085

AV² by Weigl brings you media enhanced books that support active learning.

Published by AV² by Weigl
350 5th Avenue, 59th Floor New York, NY 10118
Website: www.av2books.com www.weigl.com

Library of Congress Cataloging-in-Publication Data
Carr, Aaron.
 Bird / Aaron Carr.
    p. cm. -- (I love my pet)
 ISBN 978-1-61690-919-2 (hardcover : alk. paper) -- ISBN 978-1-61690-565-1 (online)
1. Cage birds--Juvenile literature. I. Title.
 SF461.35.C37 2011
 636.6'8--dc23
                           2011024915

Printed in the United States of America in North Mankato, Minnesota
1 2 3 4 5 6 7 8 9 0 15 14 13 12 11

062011
WEP030611

2

Project Coordinator: Aaron Carr   Art Director: Terry Paulhus
Weigl acknowledges Getty Images, iStock, and Dreamstime as image suppliers for this title.

I Love My Pet
BIRD

CONTENTS

3

I love my pet bird.
I take good care of him.

4

5

My pet bird was a chick.
He did not have any feathers
when he was born.

7

8

My pet bird grows fast.
He will be big
in about one year.

10

My pet bird has very light feathers. They help him fly.

Most birds have thousands of feathers.

My pet bird has feathers
that fall out each year.
New feathers grow
to take their place.

13

14

My pet bird
can turn his head backward.
This lets him see behind him.

My pet bird
eats many times a day.
I give him food and water
every day.

Eating apple seeds
can make birds sick.

My pet bird
likes to have a bath every day.
I keep his bath water clean.

19

20

I make sure my pet bird is healthy.
I love my pet bird.

BIRD FACTS

This page provides more detail about the interesting facts found in the book.
Simply look for the corresponding page number to match the fact.

Pages 4–5

I love my pet bird. I take good care of him. Birds come in many shapes, colors, and sizes. There are more than 9,000 types of bird. In the United States, there are about 50 million pet birds. Keeping a pet bird is a big responsibility. Some birds can live up to 100 years. Birds need regular feeding and care, including cage cleaning.

Pages 6–7

My pet bird was a chick. He did not have any feathers when he was born. Baby birds are called chicks. Some chicks are born with feathers and can walk right away. Others are born with no feathers and cannot see. After two weeks, most chicks are covered with soft feathers called down. Always be gentle when handling a chick.

Pages 8–9

My pet bird grows fast. He will be big in about one year. Most birds reach adulthood within one year. Others take two or three years to mature. Many birds leave the nest after a few weeks. Birds usually have to stay with their mother for the first 12 to 16 weeks of life. Birds have to be weaned before people can take them home.

Pages 10–11

My pet bird has very light feathers. They help him fly. Birds are the only animals that have feathers. The shape and light weight of feathers helps birds fly. Feathers also help birds stay warm and blend into their surroundings. Most birds are covered with thousands of feathers. A song bird can have between 2,000 and 4,000 feathers.

Pages 12–13

My pet bird has feathers that fall out each year. New feathers grow to take their place. Birds molt at least once each year. A bird's feathers wear out over time. During molting, birds shed their old feathers and grow new ones. Molting can be stressful for birds. Help your bird by providing plenty of fresh water and many baths.

Pages 14–15

My pet bird can turn his head backward. This lets him see behind him. Some birds, such as the owl, can almost turn their heads 360 degrees. Some birds cannot move their eyes. They can only look around by moving their head. Approaching your bird from outside of its field of vision and loud noises may scare him.

Pages 16–17

My pet bird eats many times a day. I give him food and water every day. Most birds eat little meals throughout the day. Birds eat different kinds of food depending on the type of beak they have. Birds should also eat fruits and vegetables. Talk to a breeder or veterinarian to determine the proper diet for your bird.

Pages 18–19

My pet bird likes to have a bath every day. I keep his bath water clean. Birds need to bathe often to stay healthy. Keep a bowl of water in your bird's cage. The bowl should be big enough for the bird to stand in and splash water on itself. Be careful not to put too much water in the bowl. Birds can drown in shallow water.

Pages 20–21

I help make sure my pet bird is healthy. I love my pet bird. Keep your bird's cage away from drafts, extreme heat, direct sunlight, and loud noises. Check your bird's behavior and appearance often. If you notice changes in his eating and sleeping habits, activity level, temper, or weight, take your bird to a veterinarian.

WORD LIST

Research has shown that as much as 65 percent of all written material published in English is made up of 300 words. These 300 words cannot be taught using pictures or learned by sounding them out. They must be recognized by sight. This book contains 56 common sight words to help young readers improve their reading fluency and comprehension. This book also teaches young readers several important content words, such as proper nouns. These words are paired with pictures to aid in learning and improve understanding.

Page	Sight Words First Appearance
4	good, him, I, my, of, take
6	a, any, did, have, he, not, was, when
9	about, be, big, grow, in, one, will, year
11	has, help, light, most, they, very
12	each, new, out, place, that, their, to
15	can, head, his, lets, see, this, turn
17	and, day, eats, every, food, give, make, many, times, water
18	every, keep, likes
21	is

Page	Content Words First Appearance
4	bird, pet
6	chick, feathers
15	head
17	apple seeds
18	bath

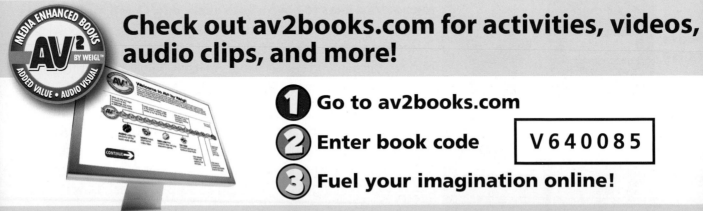

Check out av2books.com for activities, videos, audio clips, and more!

1 Go to av2books.com

2 Enter book code   V 6 4 0 0 8 5

3 Fuel your imagination online!

www.av2books.com